THE MAN WHO INVENTED THE FERRIS WHEEL

The Genius of George Ferris

Titles in the *Genius Inventors and Their Great Ideas* Series:

THE MAN WHO INVENTED THE FERRIS WHEEL

The Genius of George Ferris

By Dani Sneed

Enslow Elementary

an imprint of

Enslow Publishers, Inc.

40 Industrial Road
Box 398
Berkeley Heights, NJ 07922
USA

http://www.enslow.com

Content Advisors

James G. Ferris
Great-Great Nephew of
George Washington Gale Ferris, Jr.

Norman D. Anderson
Professor Emeritus of Science Education,
North Carolina State University
Author of *Ferris Wheel: An Illustrated History*

Series Literacy Consultant

Allan A. De Fina, Ph.D.
Past President of the New Jersey Reading Association
Chairperson, Department of Literacy Education
New Jersey City University

Enslow Elementary, an imprint of Enslow Publishers, Inc.
Enslow Elementary® is a registered trademark of Enslow Publishers, Inc.

Original edition published as *Ferris Wheel! George Ferris and His Amazing Invention* in 2008.

Library of Congress Cataloging-in-Publication Data

Sneed, Dani.
 The man who invented the ferris wheel : the genius of George Ferris / by Danell Dykstra.
  p. cm.— (Genius inventors and their great ideas)
  Includes bibliographical references and index.
 ISBN 978-0-7660-4136-3
 1. Ferris, George Washington Gale, 1859-1896—Juvenile literature. 2. Structural engineers—United States—Biography—uvenile literature. 3. Civil engineers—United States—Biography—Juvenile literature. 4. Inventors—United States—Biography—Juvenile literature. 5. Ferris wheels—History—Juvenile literature. I. Title.
 TA140.F455D95 2013
 624.1092—dc23
 [B]

                                                              2012013976

Future editions:
Paperback ISBN: 978-1-4644-0206-7
Single-User PDF ISBN: 978-1-4646-1119-3

EPUB ISBN: 978-1-4645-1119-6
Multi-User PDF ISBN: 978-0-7660-5748-7

Printed in the United States of America.

042014 Lake Book Manufacturing, Inc., Melrose Park, IL

10 9 8 7 6 5 4 3 2

To Our Readers: We have done our best to make sure all Internet addresses in this book were active and appropriate when we went to press. However, the author and the publisher have no control over and assume no liability for the material available on those Internet sites or on other Web sites they may link to. Any comments or suggestions can be sent by e-mail to comments@enslow.com or to the address on the back cover.

♻ Enslow Publishers, Inc., is committed to printing our books on recycled paper. The paper in every book contains 10% to 30% post-consumer waste (PCW). The cover board on the outside of each book contains 100% PCW. Our goal is to do our part to help young people and the environment too!

Photo Credits: Artville, p. 9; Chicago History Museum, pp. 3, 5, (bottom) 14 (ICHi-10257), 21, (ICHi-02440), 24 (ICHi-02436), 32 (ICHi-21713), 34 (ICHi-00018), 35 (ICHi-00027), 37 (ICHi-17398); Harper's Weekly, August 5, 1893, p. 30; © 2007 Jupiterimages Corporation, pp. 6, 13, 15, 38; Library of Congress, pp. 8, 11, 14; Photographic Collection, Institute of Archives and Special Collections, Rensselaer Polytechnic Institute, Troy, NY, pp. 12 (AC20); 16 (AC20); Scientific American, July 1, 1893, p. 25; Shutterstock.com, p.10, 41, 42, 43; Smithsonian Institution Libraries, Hubert Howe Bancroft, p. 31. Tom Hoffman, p. 5 (top)

Cover Photo: Chicago History Museum ICHi-10257, (Portrait of George Ferris); ©2007 Jupiterimages Corporation, (Ferris Wheel).

CONTENTS

More than two hundred million people have visited the Eiffel Tower since it was completed in 1889.

Chapter 1

A Dreamer Is Born

In 1889 crowds were amazed by the 984-foot Eiffel Tower at the Paris World's Fair. The tower was like an iron bridge to the sky. Four years later Chicago planned to have the next World's Fair. American engineers competed in a nationwide contest for an idea to outdo the French Eiffel Tower. The boldest ideas were for taller towers. Then one engineer had a different idea. George Ferris drew plans for a 250-foot wheel that could carry over two thousand people high into the sky. It seemed like a fantasy. Could George design and build such a wheel?

George Washington Gale Ferris, Jr. was born on February 14, 1859, on a farm in Galesburg, Illinois. Martha

OPENING OF THE WORLD'S FAIR

PRESIDENT CLEVELAND

Grover Cleveland was president of the United States when the 1893 World's Fair opened in Chicago, Illinois.

Ferris, his mother, named him after his father. He was their ninth child.

Five years later George's family sold their dairy farm to move west. They crossed the country in a horse-drawn coach and several wagons to Carson City, Nevada. Young George loved ranching, horses, lassos, and especially boots with spurs. He thought ranching was the best job to have.

Near George's home on the Carson River, a huge mill wheel very slowly turned in the river. The wheel lifted buckets of water and dumped the water into a tub. Horses and mules drank the cool water. Young George watched the huge wheel with

In 1864, George's family moved west from Galesburg, Illinois, to Carson City, Nevada.

Some people think George got his idea by watching a water wheel near his home.

George Ferris grew up near Carson City, Nevada.

much delight. Legend has it that he dreamed of riding on the waterwheel.

As a teen George went to the California Military Academy in Oakland, California. He then continued his education at Rensselaer Polytechnic Institute (RPI) in Troy, New York.

George's Ninth Street Bridge crossed the Allegheny River in Pittsburgh, Pennsylvania.

George enjoyed attending RPI. He was voted class president, sang in the choir, joined the rifle club, and played on the baseball team. His oldest sister, Margaret, helped by sending him money. He wrote to her saying that he was "anxious to finish" his schooling. He promised to pay back the money.

George graduated from RPI as a civil engineer in 1881. Just as he had promised, he paid back his sister with money he made designing and building train tracks, tunnels, and bridges. Two of the bridges he built were made with an amazingly strong new metal—steel. Soon George became a steel expert.

Chapter 2

A Wheel Idea

For George, 1886 was a big year. He married Margaret Ann Beatty, a pretty brunette from Canton, Ohio. He also started his own steel business, G.W.G. Ferris & Company, in Pittsburgh, Pennsylvania.

By 1890 Chicago buzzed with excitement as it planned the World's Fair. Three years before at the Paris World's Fair, all were astonished by the Eiffel Tower. The construction chief of the fair, Daniel Burnham, started a contest for an idea to outdo the tower.

George traveled to Chicago. He heard Burnham speak about the contest to engineers, who all wanted to build taller towers. Mr. Burnham asked, "What's wrong with you scientists? Towers of various kinds have been

George knew how to build bridges. He thought of his wheel as a big round bridge.

In an interview George Ferris compared hi
to a tiny wheel inside a watch that "flicks b
His point was that all wheels work the same way.

A Ferris Wheel can be compared to a bicycle wheel.
Both are tension wheels. The main difference between the
two is that a bicycle wheel rests on its outer rim while a
Ferris wheel hangs by its axle in the center. On the Ferris
wheel, each spoke on the bottom half of the wheel
is in tension. That means the hanging
wheel pulls on the spokes. As it turns,
different spokes hold up the wheel.
Each spoke supports a small
fraction of the total wheel weight.
Because there are so many spokes,
each one can be very thin.

Bicycle spokes are made of strong steel wire. They work together to
support the weight of the rider as the wheels turn.

proposed, but towers are not original." George accepted the challenge to build something different.

While eating dinner with other engineers in Chicago, George said he "hit upon the idea." He began drawing what he called a "monster wheel." He decided on

William Gronau, George's friend, also went to RPI.

details like the size of the wheel and the cost of a ticket. George, a bridge builder, was basically planning a big round tension bridge.

His friends at the table all agreed that a 250-foot-tall monster wheel would never work. They thought a wheel that big would break under its own weight.

George did not give up. He showed his idea to his friend William Gronau. The monster wheel would be a tension wheel with spokes like a bicycle. George wanted to be sure the wheel wouldn't crumple in rain, wind, or ice. William calculated the safety of the wheel when loaded with the weight of more than two thousand riders. The math showed it would work.

A determined George took his plans to Daniel Burnham. George's idea was not a taller tower. It was original.

Burnham shook his head. "Your wheel is so flimsy it would collapse, and even if it didn't, the public would be afraid to ride in it," the fair's construction chief said.

Daniel Burnham was a famous architect. He created building plans for parts of many cities.

George Ferris began rolling up his drawings. "You are an architect, sir, I am an engineer, and my wheel represents strictly an engineering problem. The spokes may seem flimsy, but they are more than strong enough." He tucked his drawings under his arm, then softly added, "I feel that no man should prejudge another man's idea unless he knows what he's talking about."

"Let me have your drawings, Mr. Ferris," Burnham said, smiling. He gave them to the World's Fair directors to look at. But the directors decided against a wheel for the fair. They were sure it could not withstand Lake

Michigan's strong winds. People started calling George's plan "G.W.'s Cockeyed Dream."

George's wheel was still a dream. But as an engineer, he knew how to design and build ideas from a dream. He would make his wheel real.

Chapter 3

Racing to Build the Wheel

In November 1892, the World's Fair directors still had nothing to beat the Eiffel Tower. They finally agreed to let George build his wheel. But he would have to pay for the wheel himself and get it done in time for the fair's opening on May 1, 1893.

George needed $400,000. He asked bank after bank to lend him money to build a 250-foot wheel. He was laughed back into the street.

Even without the money, George boldly ordered the parts he needed. Next, with the help of friends, George found some wealthy investors for the wheel. The investors said the wheel should be called the Ferris Wheel and not the Monster Wheel. George agreed.

In January, George hired a crew to dig eight holes for the concrete base. The wheel full of riders would weigh more than 2 million pounds. It needed a very solid base to hold it up. The crew chopped the frozen ground, and then dug through sand. They finally hit rock thirty-five feet down.

It was too cold for pouring the concrete foundation. Ice covered the ground. As the concrete was poured it froze before it hardened. There was no time to wait for warmer weather. The fair would open soon. What could George do? He piped steam into the concrete. Finally, the concrete hardened.

Five freight trains chugged into the construction site carrying more than 4 million pounds of steel. Two towers were built to hold the wheel. Cranes lifted the axle up to the top of the towers and settled it between them. At the time, the axle was the largest piece of steel ever forged in the United States.

To the clanking of tools and squeaking of bolts, the first section of the wheel was hung by its spokes. Then each

The axle of the first Ferris Wheel weighed about fifty tons. Here workers posed for a picture as they prepared to lift it 140 feet to the tops of the towers.

section, shaped like a piece of pie, was added. Soon it was time for the last section. Would it fit perfectly? To George's relief, it did.

Two powerful 1,000-horsepower engines were installed under the wooden platform that was built for riders to get onto the wheel. Only one engine was needed to turn the wheel. George put in two as a safety precaution. If one engine broke then the other engine could turn the wheel and bring people safely back down.

George knew just one mistake could mean disaster, but he was determined to keep going. As soon as the wheel was hung, George, who was in Pittsburgh at the time, sent a message saying "turn the wheel or tear it off at the towers." Several brave workers took a free first ride, clinging to the wheel. The fair had already opened, and people strolling among the exhibits stopped and watched in awe as the huge wheel spun around.

George's friend William Gronau watched the wheel's first turn. William sent a message to George, saying, "I could

The Ferris Wheel was built inside a giant framework, seen here.

Workers began hanging the carriages only a few days before the Ferris Wheel officially opened.

have yelled aloud for joy!" George's experiment worked. The wheel turned trouble-free. The people who had called his plan cockeyed were wrong. Racing to finish construction, George messaged back telling the crew to work day and night to hang the carriages.

On June 10 the crew began hanging the thirty-six carriages. Each wooden carriage could hold sixty people and had ten glass windows on both sides. Iron grills covered the windows because George didn't want to risk someone falling out.

With the wheel not yet finished, George boldly mailed two thousand cards to family and friends inviting them for a free ride on the wheel's opening day.

Many people still thought the wheel was unsafe. Newspaper reporters compared the spokes to a spider's web. Would anyone dare to ride the Ferris Wheel?

Chapter 4

Queen of the Midway

At three o'clock on June 21, 1893, a big brass band played "America" from a carriage high on the wheel. Flags flew. Banners of stars and stripes hung from each carriage. A crowd gathered. George gave a speech from the platform. He thanked his wife, Margaret, for encouraging him. The crowd cheered, and Margaret handed him a golden whistle. George blew loudly to signal the first ride. Men in blue coats and white pants opened the doors to the six lowest carriages. George, Margaret, and the mayor of Chicago joined the excited guests to enjoy the ride.

Filled to the limit, 2,160 people could ride the wheel at a time. After taking twenty minutes to spin around once, the wheel stopped and the conductor called, "All out."

The Ferris Wheel opened for business on June 21, 1893. It was 250 feet across.

Not only did people dare to ride the Ferris Wheel, they waited in line to do so. Couples were begging to be married at the top. George said no, but offered them his office instead. The wheel was soon called "Queen of the Midway."

Two quarters could buy someone ten rides on the carousel, but only one ride on the Ferris Wheel. The high price didn't keep children or adults off the Ferris Wheel. From eight o'clock in the morning until eleven o'clock at night, people came to ride. To make nighttime rides magical, George outlined the wheel with another new invention— light bulbs.

The fair closed on October 30, 1893. Another city would host the next World's Fair. The wheel stopped spinning for the winter.

Iron bars on the windows prevented riders from falling out of the carriages.

A ride on the Ferris Wheel cost fifty cents, which was also how much it cost to get into the fair.

About 1.5 million people rode the Ferris Wheel at the fair.

Chapter 5

The Wheel Stops Turning

In the spring of 1894 George hired a crew to take down the wheel. It took them three months to unbolt the wheel, number each piece, and load them onto a train's flatcars. The wheel spent the rest of that year on a railroad track in Chicago.

George considered what to do with his wheel. Coney Island, New York, and even London wanted the wheel. In early1895, George decided to set the wheel spinning again in a Chicago park on North Clark Street. Stoves were added to each carriage for cozy winter rides. Even so, there were too few riders. The Ferris Wheel was costing more to run than it earned in ticket sales. George finally ran out of money and had to sell his wheel. The

This photo shows the wheel being set up on North Clark Street in Chicago.

Not enough people came to ride the Ferris Wheel on North Clark Street. It was costing too much to run.

Chicago House Wrecking Company, a scrap metal company, bought the wheel for $1,800.

Things were taking a bad turn for George. He owed money. After a disagreement, his wife, Margaret, went home to her family in Ohio. Then just before Thanksgiving, George Ferris became very ill. He checked in to Mercy Hospital in Pittsburgh. Five days later, on November 28, 1896, George died. History doesn't reveal what sickness George died from, but overwork and wheel worries had definitely hurt his health.

George's Ferris Wheel enjoyed one last fling. The Chicago House Wrecking Company had not sold the metal as scrap. Instead they moved the Ferris Wheel to St. Louis, Missouri, for the 1904 World's Fair. It was again enjoyed by many. But when the fair closed, some people in St. Louis complained that the Ferris Wheel was ugly. They wanted it removed. No other large fairs were being planned at that time. On May 11, 1906, a hundred pounds of dynamite were exploded under the

After the World's Fair in St. Louis, the Ferris Wheel was scrapped.

Today, the London Eye in London, England, is one of the world's most famous Ferris wheels. About ten thousand people ride it each day.

foundation of George's wheel. Then the steel was sold for scrap metal.

No tombstone, patent, or fortune bears his name. But don't feel sorry for George. His name remains famous. Because George dared to dream big and follow his dream, today millions of people all over the world have a great time riding Ferris wheels.

TIMELINE

1859—Born on February 14 on a farm in Galesburg, Illinois.

1864—Moves to a ranch near Carson City, Nevada.

1876—Graduates from the California Military Academy.

1881—Earns a degree in Civil Engineering from Rensselaer Polytechnic Institute.

1886—Starts steel business, G.W.G. Ferris & Company, and marries Margaret Ann Beatty.

1892—Attends overseeing Chicago World's Fair engineering meeting and is inspired to design something original to rival the Eiffel Tower. Draws his concept of the Monster Wheel.

1893—Begins overseeing construction of the Ferris Wheel in January. Opens the Ferris Wheel to the Chicago World's Fair in june. Fair closes in October.

1895—Ferris Wheel turns again on North Clark Street in Chicago.

1896—Dies on November 22 in Pittsburgh, Pennsylvania.

1904—Ferris Wheel set up for the last time at the St. Louis World's Fair.

1906—Ferris Wheel is destroyed on May 11.

YOU BE THE INVENTOR!

So you want to be an inventor? You can do it! First, you need a terrific idea.

Got a problem? No problem!

Many inventions begin when someone thinks of a great solution to a problem. One cold day in 1994, 10-year-old K.K. Gregory was building a snow fort. Soon, she had snow between her mittens and her coat sleeve. Her wrists were cold and wet. She found some scraps of fabric around the house, and used them to make a tube that would fit around her wrist. She cut a thumbhole in the tube to make a kind of fingerless glove, and called it a "Wristie." Wearing mittens over her new invention, her wrists stayed nice and warm when she played outside. Today, the Wristie business is booming.

Now it's your turn. Maybe, like K.K. Gregory, you have an idea for something new that would make your life better or easier. Perhaps you can think of a way improve an everyday item. Twelve year-old Becky Schroeder became the youngest female ever to receive a U.S. patent after she invented a glow-in-the dark clipboard that allowed people to write in the dark. Do you like to play sports or board games? James Naismith, inspired by a game he used to play as a boy, invented a new game he called basketball.

Let your imagination run wild. You never know where it will take you.

Research it!

Okay, you have a terrific idea for an invention. Now what?

First, you'll want to make sure that nobody else has thought of your idea. You wouldn't want to

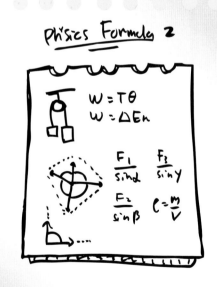

spend hours developing your new invention, only to find that someone else beat you to it. Google Patents can help you find out whether your idea is original.

Bring it to life!

If no one else has thought of your idea, congratulations! Write it down in a logbook or journal. Write the date and your initials for every entry you make. If you file a patent for your invention later, this will help you prove that you were the first person to think of it. The most important thing about this logbook is that pages cannot be added or subtracted. You can buy a bound notebook at any office supply store.

Draw several different pictures of your invention in your logbook. Try sketching views from above, below, and to the side. Show how big each part of your invention should be.

Build a model. Don't be discouraged if it doesn't work at first. You may have to experiment with different designs and materials. That's part of the fun! Take pictures of everything, and tape them into your logbook.

Try your invention out on your friends and family. If they have any suggestions to make it better, build another model. Perfect your invention, and give it a clever name.

Patent it!

Do you want to sell your invention? You'll want to apply for a patent. Holding a patent to your invention means that no one else can make, use, or sell your invention in the U.S. without your permission. It prevents others from making money off of your idea. You will definitely need an adult to help you apply for a patent. It can be a complicated and expensive process. But if you think that people will want to buy your invention, it is well worth it.

WORDS TO KNOW

architect—Someone who is trained to design buildings.

axle—A central rotating shaft that sends power to a wheel.

civil engineer—Someone who is trained to design and build structures like bridges and roads.

concrete—A mixture of sand, gravel, cement, and water used to build sidewalks and bases of buildings (foundations).

investor—A person who gives money for something, like starting a company, believing they will get back more money in the future.

midway—An area of a fair or carnival where rides and games are located.

patent—A legal paper that gives only the inventor the right to make and sell his or her invention.

polytechnic institute—A school that teaches industrial arts and applied sciences like engineering. "Poly" means many, and "technic" means arts.

spoke—A thin rod or wire that connects the wheel to the axle.

steel—A strong, hard metal made of iron.

tension—The tightness of a rope or wire.

LEARN MORE

Books

Alter, Judy. *Amusement Parks: Roller Coasters, Ferris Wheels, and Cotton Candy.* Danbury, Conn.: Scholastic Library Publishing, 1997.

Bodden, Valerie. *Ferris Wheels.* Mankato, Minn.: Creative Education, 2012.

Buckley, Susan. *Kids Make History: A New Look at America's Story.* New York: Houghton Mifflin Books for Children, 2006.

Kassinger, Ruth. *Iron and Steel: From Thor's Hammer to the Space Shuttle.* Minneapolis: Twenty-First Century Books, 2003.

St. George, Judith. *So You Want to Be an Inventor?* New York: Penguin, 2005.

Smith, A. G. *Cut and Assemble a Ferris Wheel.* Mineola, N.Y.: Dover Publications, Inc. 1992.

LEARN MORE

Internet Addresses

If you want to find out more about George Ferris, check out these Web sites:

Amusement Park Rides and Their Inventors
<http://inventors.about.com/>

Internet Fairground History: Ferris Wheel Research
<http://library.thinkquest.org/C002926/history/ferris1.html>

If you want to learn more about becoming an inventor, check out these Web sites:

Inventnow.org
<http://www.inventnow.org/>

Inventive Kids
<http://www.inventivekids.com/>

The U.S. Patent and Trademark Office For Kids
<http://www.uspto.gov/kids/>

INDEX